HOW MACHINES WORK

EMERGENCY VEHICLES

IAN GRAHAM

W

FRANKLIN WATTS

LONDON • SYDNEY

 An Appleseed Editions book

First published in 2008 by Franklin Watts

Franklin Watts
338 Euston Road, London NW1 3BH

Franklin Watts Australia
Level 17/207 Kent St, Sydney, NSW 2000

© 2008 Appleseed Editions

Appleseed Editions Ltd
Well House, Friars Hill, Guestling, East Sussex TN35 4ET

Created by Q2AMedia
Series Editor: Honor Head
Book Editor: Harriet McGregor
Senior Art Director: Ashita Murgai
Designer: Harleen Mehta, Ravijot Singh
Picture Researcher: Amit Tigga

ISBN 978 0 7496 8079 4

Dewey classification: 629.225

All words in **bold** can be found in Glossary on pages 30–31.

Website information is correct at time of going to press. However, the publishers cannot
accept liability for any information or links found on third-party websites.

A CIP catalogue for this book is available from the British Library.

Picture credits
t=top b=bottom c=centre l=left r=right m=middle
Cover Images: © 2007 theflightcollection.com

Mark Boulton/ Alamy: 4, Brian Finestone/ Shutterstock: 5t, David R Frazier/ Photolibrary: 5b, Van Hilversum/ Alamy: 6,
Blue Shadows/ Alamy: 7b, Stockfolio/ Alamy: 8, Chris Herring/ Alamy: 9b, Osh kosh Truck Corporation: 10–13,
Sylvia Cordaiy Photo Library Ltd/ Alamy: 14, US Navy: 15, Corbis: 16, Michael Donne/ SPL/ Photolibrary: 16b,
Associated Press: 17, Dodmedia: 18, Royal Navy/ epa/ Corbis: 19b, Dodmedia: 20–21, Ford Media: 22, Associated Press: 23,
Sean Murphy/ Gettyimages: 24, Gary Sludden/Istockphoto: 25t, Dave Penman/ Rex Features: 25b, Dodmedia: 26,
Alain Le Bot/ Photononstop/ Photolibrary: 27, Jacob Halaska/ Index Stock Imagery/ Photolibrary: 28,
Michael Donne/ Science Photo Library/ Photolibrary: 29

Q2AMedia Art Bank: 7t, 9t, 15t, 19t

Printed in Hong Kong

Franklin Watts is a division of Hachette Children's Books

CONTENTS

Emergency Vehicles   4

Firefighting Vehicles   6

Airport Emergency!   10

Rescue at Sea   14

Deep-sea Rescue   18

Police Cars   22

Ambulances   26

Glossary   30

Index and Websites   32

EMERGENCY VEHICLES

When an accident happens, or when people are injured, it is vital to get help to the scene as quickly as possible. This is when emergency vehicles are needed.

SPECIAL EQUIPMENT

Emergency vehicles come in all shapes and sizes. They can travel fast by land, sea or air – even underwater. They carry equipment for dealing with all kinds of emergencies. Some are equipped to search for missing people and rescue them. Others take care of sick and injured people. Firefighting vehicles carry everything needed for putting out fires.

Water/foam mixture sprayed onto flames from above

Firefighters tackle a blaze from a platform mounted on a **hydraulic** ladder

▲ Aircraft are the fastest emergency vehicles. This helicopter ambulance can quickly reach the scene of an accident when roads are blocked by ice and snow

RADIO CONTACT

In an emergency, rescuers need to know what is going on. All emergency vehicles have radios to allow rescue teams to keep in touch with base and with each other. The vehicles are called into action by radio. Police cars also have radios so officers out on patrol can report back to base.

◀ A police officer in a patrol car talks to base by radio

FIREFIGHTING VEHICLES

There are many different types of firefighting vehicles. Fire engines, ladder trucks, rescue vehicles and water tankers all work together to help put out fires.

A fire engine is a truck with a powerful pump which forces water through hoses to put out flames. The pump is powered by the vehicle's engine. A fire engine's own water tank soon runs out, but it can use water sucked up from a river, piped from a tanker truck or supplied from an underground pipe by a **hydrant**.

▼ On board a fire engine, equipment and protective gear is stored in special lockers

Safety helmets and protective clothing

Hose reels and **nozzles**

Foam mixture for tackling oil and petrol fires

MECHANICAL MUSCLES

Raising and extending a heavy fire engine ladder takes enormous force. Powerful mechanical pushers called hydraulic rams do this job. Oil pumped into a cylinder pushes a rod, or ram, which raises the ladder.

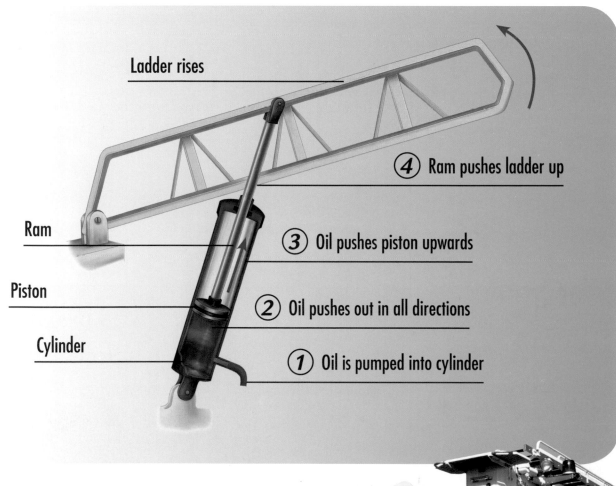

Ladder rises

Ram

Piston

Cylinder

④ Ram pushes ladder up

③ Oil pushes piston upwards

② Oil pushes out in all directions

① Oil is pumped into cylinder

▲ A **hydraulic cylinder** uses high-pressure oil to push upwards with great force

Hydrant

▶ A fire hydrant supplies water to a fire truck

FIREFIGHTING AIRCRAFT

Big forest fires are hard to fight on the ground. The scene of the fire may be difficult to reach by road, and there may be no rivers or lakes nearby to supply water to fire trucks. Fires like these are often fought from the air by helicopters and planes. The aircraft 'bomb' the fire with lots of water or water/foam mixture. The water is stored in tanks which can be filled quickly and emptied even faster.

▼ A Bombardier 415 firefighting plane waterbombs a burning forest

Water released from tanks in belly of plane

BOMBARDIER 415

Specification

Engines:	Pratt & Whitney turboprops
Size:	775 kw (1,039 hp)
Top speed:	376 kph (233 mph)
Tank capacity:	61,60 l

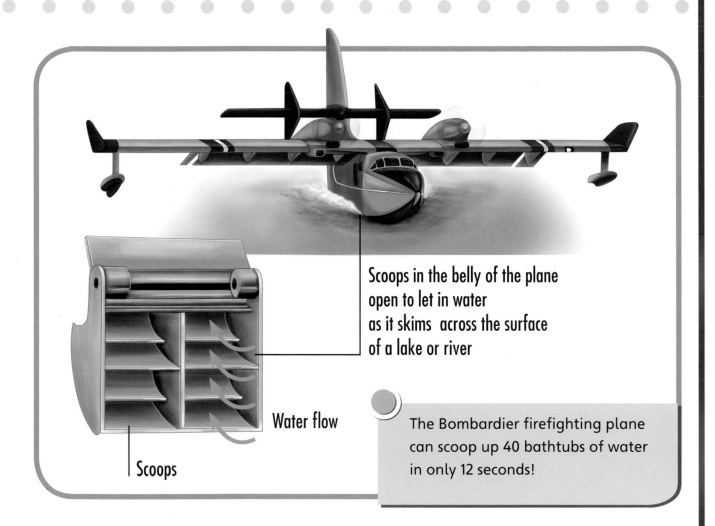

Scoops in the belly of the plane
open to let in water
as it skims across the surface
of a lake or river

Water flow

Scoops

The Bombardier firefighting plane
can scoop up 40 bathtubs of water
in only 12 seconds!

FILLING UP

Firefighting planes are designed to be able to land on water.
To fill their tanks, they swoop down onto lakes or rivers. As they
skim across the water's surface, scoops in the bottom of the
plane open and water floods in. Then, without stopping, the
planes take off again and fly back to the scene of the fire.

▶ A firefighting
helicopter fills its
tanks by sucking water
up through a pipe
called a **snorkel**

Snorkel

AIRPORT EMERGENCY

Large airports have special vehicles for fighting aircraft fires. They have to move fast and to carry everything needed to deal with burning planes.

AIRPORT FIRE ENGINES

Airport fire trucks are known as ARFFs (Airport Rescue and Fire Fighting vehicles). They have to carry more water than an ordinary fire engine because there is usually no other water supply nearby. They also have to pump water out fast to deal with big fires.

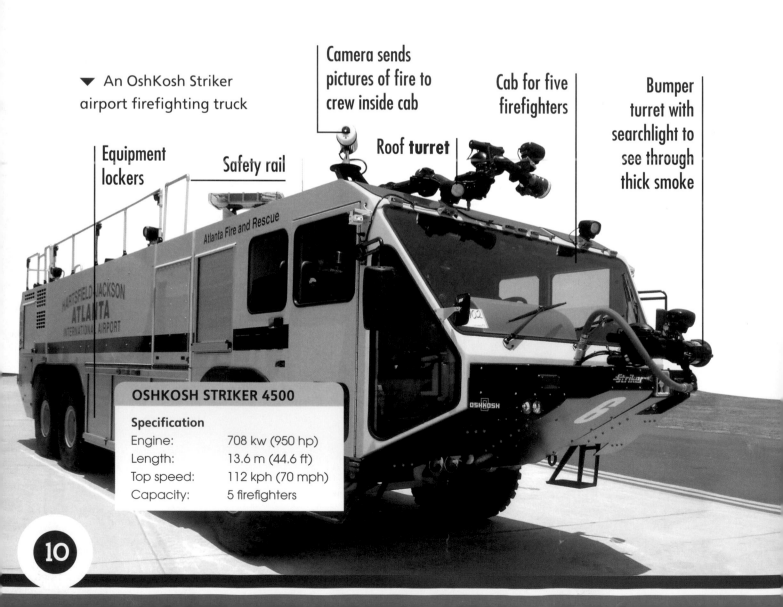

▼ An OshKosh Striker airport firefighting truck

Camera sends pictures of fire to crew inside cab

Cab for five firefighters

Bumper turret with searchlight to see through thick smoke

Equipment lockers

Safety rail

Roof **turret**

Atlanta Fire and Rescue

HARTSFIELD JACKSON ATLANTA INTERNATIONAL AIRPORT

OSHKOSH STRIKER 4500

Specification
Engine: 708 kw (950 hp)
Length: 13.6 m (44.6 ft)
Top speed: 112 kph (70 mph)
Capacity: 5 firefighters

▼ Airport firefighters spray foam on burning aircraft fuel during a training exercise

Spray gun mounted on flexible **cherry picker**

PUMPING FOAM

Fires caused by burning aircraft fuel cannot be put out by water. The fuel just floats to the surface and carries on burning. Airport fire engines can spray either water or foam. Foam settles on top of burning fuel like a blanket and smothers it. The biggest airport fire trucks can carry more than 17,000 litres of water and 2,300 litres of foam.

Spray guns on the outside of the fire truck are controlled by joysticks inside the cab

Joystick

▼ The Striker fire truck will stay upright even when tilted at an angle of 30 degrees!

INSIDE THE CAB

If a fire is very dangerous, airport firefighters may need to tackle it from inside the cab. They can do this by spraying water or foam onto the flames by **remote control**. Nozzles, called turrets, are mounted on the truck's roof and front bumper. The nozzles are steered by joysticks inside the driver's cab.

PUNCHING THROUGH METAL

When a plane is on fire, airport firefighters may need to punch through the metal body of the plane to tackle the blaze. To do this, some fire trucks use a **puncture nozzle** or piercing nozzle. This has a sharp point which is fitted to the end of the cherry picker arm on the top of the truck. The arm can also be raised high in the air to spray foam or water from above.

Piercing nozzle
For punching through metal

Camera
Sends close-up images of fire to cab

Cherry picker arm has vertical reach of 15 m

▶ The sharp point on the end of this nozzle (see inset) can punch right through the metal side of an aircraft to tackle a blaze inside the fuselage

RESCUE AT SEA

Rescues at sea are carried out by lifeboats and helicopters. Helicopters are faster than lifeboats, but lifeboats can stay out at sea for longer.

LIFEBOATS IN ACTION

When a distress call goes out, lifeboats need to get into action straight away. Small lifeboats are used for rescues near the shore and bigger, all-weather lifeboats for rescues at sea. **Inflatable** lifeboats can often be seen on holiday beaches. They are so light that they can be launched straight from the beach.

Wheelhouse
Equipped with radar, sonar and VHF direction-finding equipment

Aft cabin
Contains emergency food and medical supplies for survivors

◀ A lifeboat slides into the water down a special ramp called a slipway

STAYING AFLOAT

Lifeboats often have to go out in very bad weather. A normal boat could be pushed over by high waves and sink. Most lifeboats do not sink, because they are self-righting: if the boat rolls upside down, **buoyancy** tanks full of air in the hull of the boat turn it the right way up again.

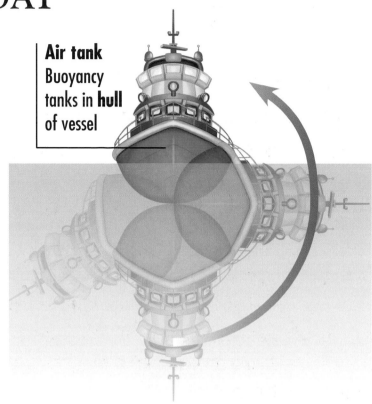

Air tank
Buoyancy tanks in **hull** of vessel

▲ With the help of its buoyancy tanks, a capsized lifeboat can right itself in just a few seconds

▼ A US Coastguard motor lifeboat ploughs through rough seas during an exercise off the Pacific coast

US Coastguard lifeboats are built to withstand waves up to 6 m high!

SEARCH AND RESCUE

Search and Rescue (SAR) helicopters look for people and boats that are in trouble out at sea. On board the helicopters are special heat-sensitive cameras to help find people at night or when bad weather makes it hard to see. The cameras detect the heat of human bodies and display this on a screen in the helicopter's cockpit.

▼ A US Coastguard helicopter **hovers** over someone in trouble in the water

▶ An observer in a search and rescue aircraft looks at images from a thermal (heat-sensing) camera. A camera like this can spot someone in the sea up to 800 m away.

◀ A survivor is lifted to safety by the crew of a rescue helicopter

Winch operator
Lowers and raises cable

This MBB Bo 105 rescue helicopter has a top speed of 242 kph. Its winch-operated hoist can lift loads of up to 272 kg

Winchman
Linked by radio to helicopter crew

Lifejacket and harness
Protect survivor from injury

DID YOU KNOW?
Since 1945, more than a million lives have been saved by helicopter rescues.

Static line
Touches water first to discharge static electricity

DEEP-SEA RESCUE

To reach people trapped underwater, special rescue vessels sometimes have to dive deep below the surface. These small diving craft are called **submersibles**.

HOW SUBMERSIBLES WORK

Submersibles are powered by electric propellers. They dive by letting seawater flood into tanks to make them heavy enough to sink. Powerful searchlights allow the crew to see through murky water. Tools on the outside of the craft, including **grippers** and cutters, are controlled by the crew from inside. The tools are used to move or cut wreckage that gets in the way.

▼ The LR5 is a British rescue submersible. It can dive to a depth of 400 m

BRITISH NAVY LRS

Specification

Propulsion:	2 propellers, 4 thrusters
Length:	9.2 m (30 ft)
Top speed:	4.6 kph (2.8 mph)
Capacity:	3 crew, 16 passengers

INSIDE A RESCUE SUB

The job of a rescue sub is to dive to a larger trapped submarine and land on its deck. A tube, called a **docking** skirt, connects the rescue sub to the large sub. Seawater is pumped out of the tube. Then the two subs open their **hatches** at each end of the tube and the crew can escape to safety on board the rescue sub.

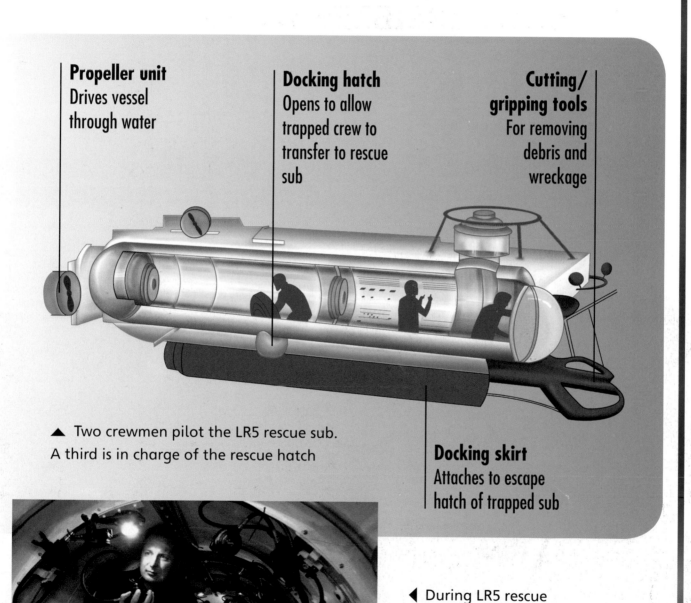

Propeller unit
Drives vessel through water

Docking hatch
Opens to allow trapped crew to transfer to rescue sub

Cutting/ gripping tools
For removing debris and wreckage

▲ Two crewmen pilot the LR5 rescue sub. A third is in charge of the rescue hatch

Docking skirt
Attaches to escape hatch of trapped sub

◀ During LR5 rescue missions, up to 16 submarine crew members can be brought to the surface inside this chamber

DEEP-DIVING SUBS

The US Navy has two deep-diving rescue subs called Deep Submergence Rescue Vehicles (DSRVs). They can dive to a depth of 1,500 m. Each sub has an arm and gripper to clear wreckage. One big propeller at the back pushes it through the water and four small battery-powered propellers, called thrusters, steer it.

US NAVY DSRV

Specification

Engine:	1 propeller, 4 thrusters
Length:	15 m
Top speed:	7.47 kph
Capacity:	4 crew, 24 passengers

▼ The US Navy's DSRV rescue sub is designed to travel piggy-back on the deck of another submarine. It can also be transported by truck, aircraft or ship

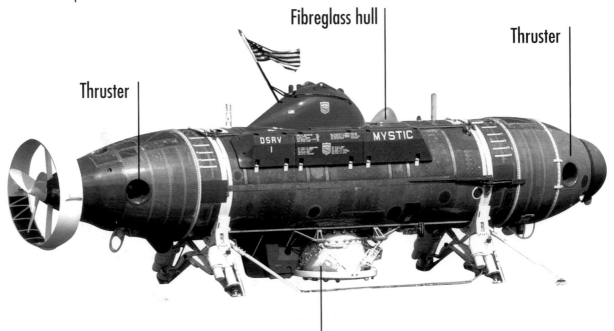

Fibreglass hull

Thruster

Thruster

Docking skirt

DIVING SUITS

Before a rescue, a diver may be sent to look at a trapped submarine. Very deep dives are made using a special metal diving suit called a **hardsuit** or atmospheric diving system. A hardsuit is a high-tech suit of armour, strong enough to resist the crushing weight of water up to 600 m below the surface. Watertight joints enable the diver to bend his arms and legs.

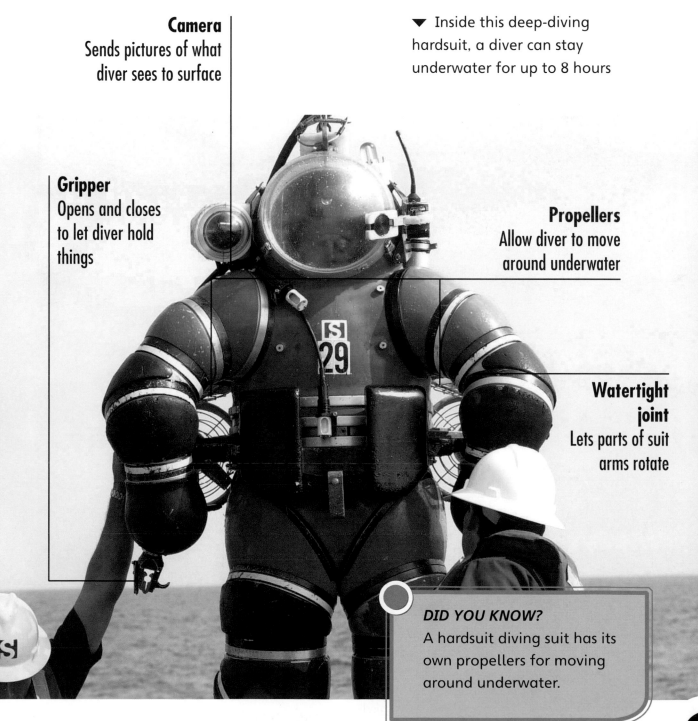

Camera
Sends pictures of what diver sees to surface

▼ Inside this deep-diving hardsuit, a diver can stay underwater for up to 8 hours

Gripper
Opens and closes to let diver hold things

Propellers
Allow diver to move around underwater

Watertight joint
Lets parts of suit arms rotate

DID YOU KNOW?
A hardsuit diving suit has its own propellers for moving around underwater.

POLICE CARS

Most of the time, police cars patrol the streets at normal speeds, but in an accident or emergency they have to be able to get to the scene – *fast!*

WHAT MAKES A CAR A POLICE CAR?

Police cars work in the same way as ordinary cars, but because of the special job they do, they have to be fitted with better brakes, springs and tyres to make them tougher and more reliable. Inside, they also have to carry all the radio, computer and video equipment that police officers need when they are out on patrol.

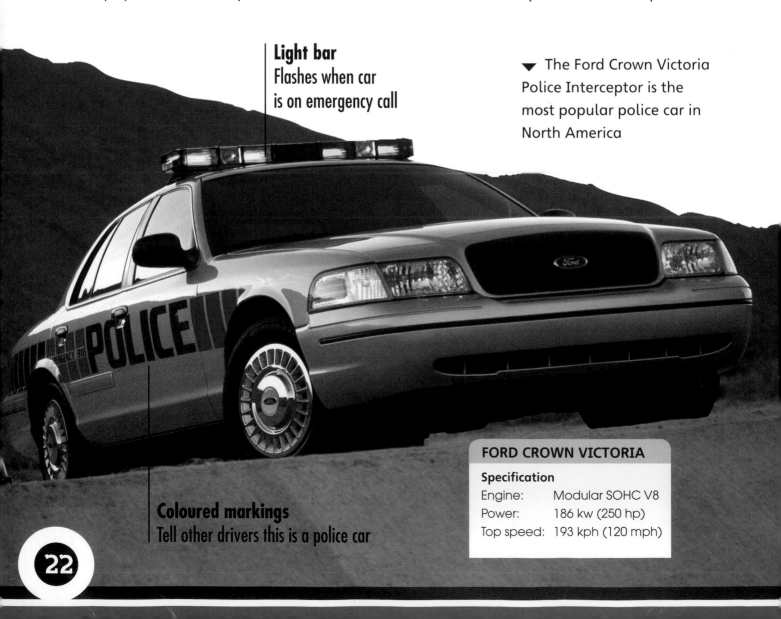

Light bar
Flashes when car is on emergency call

▼ The Ford Crown Victoria Police Interceptor is the most popular police car in North America

Coloured markings
Tell other drivers this is a police car

FORD CROWN VICTORIA

Specification

Engine:	Modular SOHC V8
Power:	186 kw (250 hp)
Top speed:	193 kph (120 mph)

▲ A police officer on patrol eyes his dashboard computer as it flashes up licence plates of passing cars

Computer **terminal** linked to main police network

INSIDE A POLICE CAR

Some police cars are equipped with computer terminals which are linked by radio to the main police computer **network**. When an officer on patrol wants to check the details of a suspicious car or person, he or she types the details on the keyboard. Within seconds, anything known about the car or person is sent back to the terminal and flashed up on screen.

MAKE WAY – POLICE!

In an emergency, police cars often have to be able to make other vehicles stop or move out of their way. In order to do this they have to be easily identified as police cars, so they are usually painted in bright colours. They also have flashing lights and loud **sirens** to warn other drivers to pull in and let them pass.

DID YOU KNOW?
Some emergency vehicles carry an EVP (Emergency Vehicle Pre-emption) device, which the crew can use to change traffic lights ahead to green!

Beacon light
Clamps magnetically to roof of car

▼ A loud siren and a magnetic warning light instantly turn this unmarked car into a police car on a high-speed chase

▼ This police helicopter is powered by two turbine engines and has eight seats for pilot and passengers

Powerful searchlight for use at night

As well as daylight and heat-sensing cameras, police helicopters have loudspeakers to broadcast information or warning messages to the public

Surveillance camera relays images to screen in helicopter cockpit and to police HQ

EYE IN THE SKY

Police helicopters are often used to hover over trouble spots and chase speeding cars or escaping criminals. As well as a normal daylight camera, a police helicopter also carries a heat-sensitive camera which can detect people and cars moving around in the dark. While the helicopter hovers overhead, the crew can guide police officers on the ground by radio.

▲ A close-up view of the helicopter's surveillance camera

AMBULANCES

Ambulances are vehicles that are specially built and equipped to carry sick and injured people to hospital. Most ambulances go by road, but some can fly!

Warning lights on all four sides of ambulance

Patient strapped to height-adjustable stretcher

▼ Paramedics carefully lift a patient on board an ambulance on a height-adjustable stretcher

Wide doors allow easy access

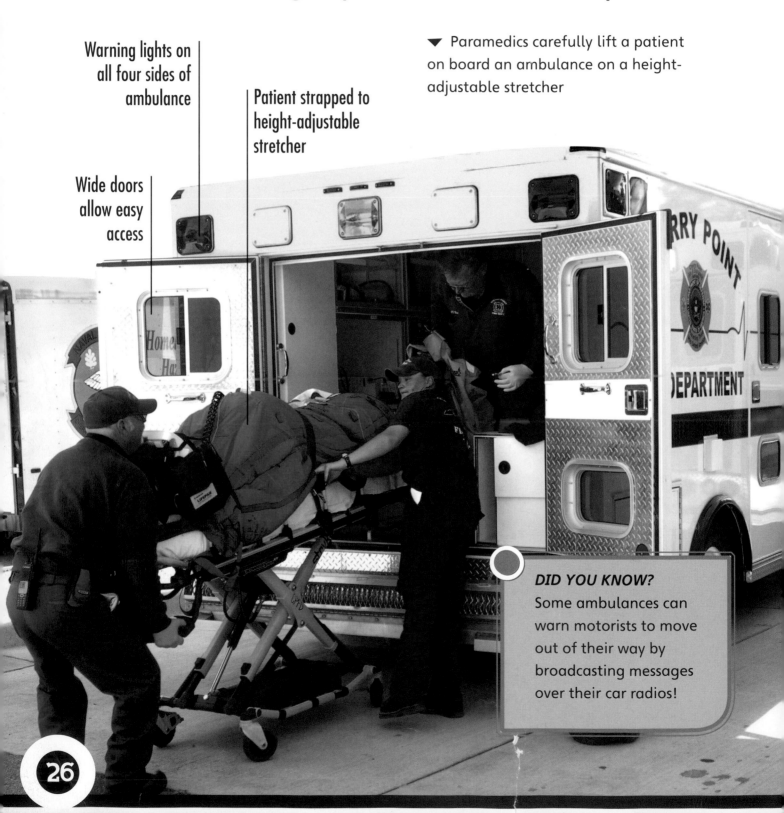

DID YOU KNOW?
Some ambulances can warn motorists to move out of their way by broadcasting messages over their car radios!

HOW AN AMBULANCE IS BUILT

Ambulances are built by attaching a specially designed vehicle body to the bottom part of a light truck. Like police cars, ambulances are painted in bright, easily recognised colours. They are also fitted with bright lights and loud sirens, so other drivers can see them and move out of their way.

INSIDE AN AMBULANCE

Paramedics have all the equipment they need to provide life-saving emergency care. Oxygen is available for people with breathing problems, and monitors allow patients' heart and pulse rates to be checked. If a patient's heart stops beating, a machine called a **defibrillator** can start it again by giving it an electric shock.

▶ An ambulance paramedic gives a patient life-saving emergency treatment

Defibrillator
Uses electrical signals to revive a patient's heart

Oxygen mask
Helps the patient breathe

27

WHAT IS AN AIR AMBULANCE?

Patients or casualties who need very urgent medical treatment may be taken to hospital in an **air ambulance**. Planes are used for long journeys, helicopters for shorter trips. A helicopter ambulance can land in a small space which may be difficult to reach by road. As soon as the casualty has been lifted on board, the helicopter can take off for a fast flight to hospital.

▼ Paramedics and crew help to lift a casualty on board an air ambulance

DID YOU KNOW?
Helicopter ambulances have been in use in the USA since 1972

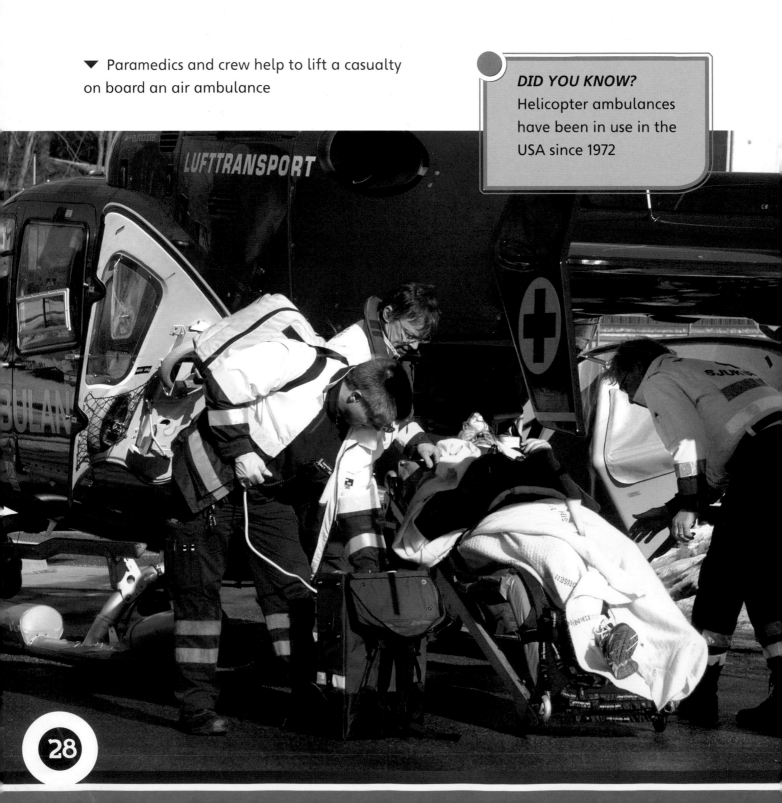

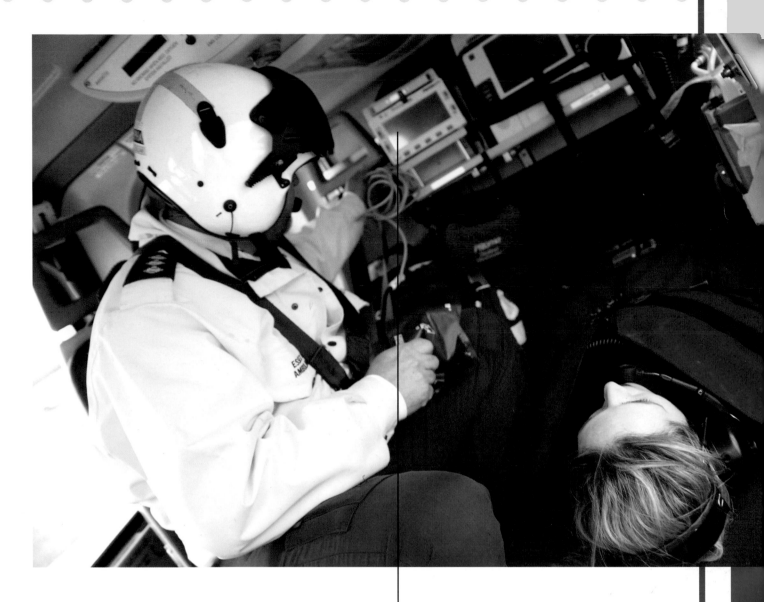

▲ A paramedic attends to a patient on board a helicopter ambulance

Monitors and emergency medical equipment allow paramedics to check the patient's condition during the flight

INSIDE AN AIR AMBULANCE

Lying on a stretcher, the patient is loaded into the aircraft through a side door or through a pair of doors at the back. Inside a helicopter ambulance, there is only just enough space for the pilot, the patient and a doctor. The rest of the space is taken up with equipment to monitor the patient's condition during the short flight to hospital.

GLOSSARY

Air ambulance
A plane or helicopter used to transport patients by air

Buoyancy The ability of a ship or boat to stay afloat in the water

Cherry picker
An extendable arm for reaching high above the ground

Defibrillator
A machine carried by ambulances for restarting a patient's heart if it stops beating

Docking Joining two craft, such as submarine and a rescue sub. Two vessels dock when they link up with each other

Gripper A robotic hand, one of the tools carried by submersibles and small robot subs for picking up and moving things underwater

Hardsuit A hard metal diving suit for very deep dives, also called an atmospheric diving system

Hatch A doorway in a ship or submarine

Hover To stay in the same spot in the air

Hull The part of a boat that sits in the water

Hydrant A water pipe coming out of the ground, used by firefighters to supply water for their hoses

Hydraulic Operated by liquid. Hydraulic machines such as fire engine ladders are operated by high-pressure oil

Hydraulic cylinder
A piece of equipment that pushes hard when high-pressure oil is pumped into it, used to raise a fire engine ladder

Inflatable A boat made of air-filled rubber

Ladder truck
A firefighting vehicle with an extending ladder on top

Monitor A screen in a hospital or an ambulance that shows information about a patient's condition

Network A group of computers that are connected electronically so that they can share information

Nozzle A metal pipe at the end of a firefighting hose where the water gushes out

Puncture nozzle A nozzle on top of an airport firefighting vehicle with a sharp, spear-shaped point for punching a hole in the side of a plane

Remote control Steering a device or machine from a distance, usually in order to keep operators out of danger

Siren A device that makes a loud noise to warn people of danger

Snorkel A pipe lowered from a firefighting helicopter to suck water up into its tanks

Submersible A small diving craft for underwater work, exploration and rescues

Terminal A computer that is linked to other computers on a network

Turret A steerable nozzle on a firefighting vehicle for spraying water or foam onto a fire

INDEX

aircraft fire 10
Airport Rescue
   and Fire Fighting
   vehicles (ARFFs) 10
ambulance 5, 26–29
atmospheric diving
   system 21

buoyancy tank 15

Deep Submergence
   Rescue Vehicles
   (DSRVs) 20

electric propeller 18

firefighting 4, 6, 8–10

gripper 18, 21

hardsuit 21
heat-sensitive
   camera 16, 25
helicopter 5, 8, 9, 14,
   16, 17, 25, 28, 29
hospital 26, 28, 29
hydrant 6, 7
hydraulic ram 7

ladder truck 6
lifeboat 14, 15

police car 5, 22–24,
   27

radio 5, 17, 22, 23, 25,
   26

Search and Rescue
   (SAR) 16, 17
siren 24, 27

tanker 6
thruster 18, 20
turret 10, 12

Websites

http://www.hoffmanestates.com/police/Insideshow.shtml
Click on the equipment inside a police car to find out what it
does.

http://www.roanoke.com/multimedia/360s/rescue.html
Take a tour of the inside of an ambulance.

http://www.merseyside.police.uk/html/aboutus/departments/
air-support/inside-copter/index.htm
Explore the cockpit and controls of a police helicopter